T0370152

THE
JEWISH VIEW
OF
ABORTION

THE
JEWISH VIEW
OF
ABORTION

INSIGHTS AND FAITH,
MISCONCEPTIONS AND REALITY

Rabbi Michael Barclay

Bartleby Press
Washington • Baltimore

Cover design by Ross Feldner

Published by
Bartleby Press
PO Box 858
Savage MD 20763
800-953-9929
Bartlebythepublisher.com

Library of Congress Control Number: 2024945335

ISBN 978-088400-404-2 (print)
ISBN 978-088400-406-6 (epub)

In honor of Iris Barclay and Rose Handler,
my mother and grandmother, of blessed memory

Contents

Preface

I grew up as a liberal Reform Jew in Southern California during the 1970's. I was raised by my parents, grandmother, and brother—all of whom are of blessed memory—to think critically and live ethically. Like most people in my demographic, I was passionate about "social justice", condemned the Republican Party as "evil," mostly because of Watergate, and somewhat blindly accepted what I read in the newspapers or saw on the television. When I went on to do my undergraduate study at U.C. Berkeley, I continued to be a "liberal" who even volunteered on political campaigns all the way through supporting Jerry Brown, the former Governor of California, in his run for the Presidency.

At the same time, I was deeply involved in both studying Judaism, Jewish mysticism, as well as the practices and beliefs of indigenous tribal cultures. The more I explored theology, the greater my understanding of life through a spiritual lens; the more tolerant I became of opposing opinions; the more I became committed to serving God; and ultimately, I enrolled in Rabbinic school to become a Rabbi. This is where my Jewish perception of the highly charged political issue of abortion developed and deepened.

In a class with Rabbi Elijah Schochet, one of the great Jewish scholars and men of our time, I started to study what traditional Judaism has taught about abortion for over 2000 years. I had been raised that abortion was actually a simple issue: Roe v. Wade was good; the debate was between "pro-life" and "pro-choice"; and that Judaism was pro-abortion. But thanks to Rabbi Schochet, who has always been committed to the idea that we can disagree without being disagreeable, I learned the truth...

I was wrong.

The issue of abortion is not a simple black and white issue, and it is, in fact, the exact opposite. There are nuances and considerations that I had never thought about personally that are vital aspects of understanding the issue. Many of the preconceptions of my youth were one dimensional, and the issue itself has many facets. I was entirely wrong about what I thought Judaism's view was about abortion.

And so, I started to explore the issue of abortion through a traditional Jewish lens. I studied texts and commentaries. I had dialogues with great Rabbis like Rabbi Shlomo "Schwartzie" Schwartz z"l and Rabbi Avraham Greenbaum. I discussed it with my wife Allison, who is always my best sounding board. When my twin sons Benjamin and Jonathan were born, I had a new awareness of the issue, now as a father. I delved deeper and deeper into how Judaism actually handles the issue of abortion, and started giving a yearly class on the topic at our synagogue, Temple Ner Simcha, where the community would ask penetrating questions that forced me to explore more of our texts and teachings on the topic.

When Jeremy Kay of Bartleby Press suggested that I take all these teachings and integrate them into a succinct book on the topic, I had to really think deeply about it. But under his guidance, I realized how necessary it was in these challenging times to write a straightforward book about abortion within the Jewish tradition. Why?

There are a multitude of reasons why this material needs to be shared, only one of them being the Dobbs decision and other political or legal considerations,

Most non-Orthodox Jews are like I was decades ago: they have been led to believe the fallacy that Judaism is pro-abortion. As a result, many non-Jews are under the same mistaken belief—a conviction that needs to be corrected. For my Christian brothers and sisters, I feel that it will radically improve inter-faith relations if an accurate accounting of the Jewish view on abortion is presented.view on abortion is presented.

For me personally, the most important reason to present this material about abortion and Judaism is to increase dialogue within the public arena about the entire issue. While the classic 20th/21st century debate on abortion is pro-life vs. pro-choice, Judaism looks at the issue from an entirely different perspective. A perspective that encourages dialogue and a deeper analysis of the issue, as opposed to the political rhetoric and extremism that is prevalent in our society. I am optimistic that by entering the traditional Jewish view of abortion into the public sphere, the discussion will come out of theology rather than out of political passions.

My deepest hope is that this material brings together people of different faith traditions in a dialogue that honors God, from whom all things come. I believe and hope that as we explore a different theology, we become closer to each other as human beings who recognize that we are all His children... that even if we disagree, we refrain from becoming disagreeable.

And now, let is explore together the topic of the Jewish perspectives on abortion...

Introduction

Abortion (often politically phrased inappropriately as "women's rights" or "reproductive rights", as it is not about a right to reproduce nor is it exclusively about the mother) is a primary political issue that is not merely divisive, it elicits passionate dialogue and sometimes even vitriol between people who were formerly friends.

A politically conservative Jew that believes that abortion should be legal in all cases but disagrees with liberal politics in every other place will often vote Democratic because of this issue of abortion. Similarly, a politically liberal Jew may vote Republican not because they agree with the majority of the Republican party's platform, but because they feel that they have a religious responsibility to protect the unborn fetus.

This book has a simple goal: to present a classic Jewish understanding of the issues surrounding abortion in an easy-to-understand format so that people can determine their position on this issue based on the dialogues and teachings of thousands of years, and without political personalities and personal passions getting in the way of that understanding.

Before even beginning to understand this complicated issue, it is important to understand a primary concept of disputation within Judaism, known as "elu v'elu". This literally means "these and these", and is a concept found in the Gemara, a part of the Talmud, where it says "these words and these words are both words of the living God."

…elu v'elu divrei Elohim chayim…
("These and also those are the
words of the living God")

This is a basic foundation stone of Judaism: the religion recognizes that no one human being can have a complete understanding of God, and so the tradition is to embrace dialogue and argumentation (known as "machlochet"). Judaism realizes that through posing questions and dialoguing with each other, a greater understanding of the infinitude of God is achieved.

This concept of elu v'elu is fundamental to Jewishly understand any topic, especially when dealing with a complicated issue such as abortion. There are many subtle points in the arguments of ancient Sages about abortion, birth control, the rights of the mother, and the rights of the fetus. To even begin to understand these arguments, in order to develop an educated opinion on the topic, we must allow ourselves to be guided by the many opinions expressed over the centuries. We must also remember that while we may ultimately disagree with another person in their personal conclusion about how abortion should or should not be used, it is imperative that we disagree without being disagreeable. Judaism is based on the process of dialogue, and we do not need to destroy a relationship with a friend because we disagree with their understanding of an issue.

Too often due to modern communication, concepts become disjointed or downright inaccurate, seemingly overnight. Jewish perspectives in the abortion debate are no different. As a result, some beliefs, even by Jews, become warped or presented inaccurately to advance a particular argument. While some may do this intentionally, most do not even realize their misconceptions.

It is because of this powerful concept of elu v'elu that we will be avoiding as much as possible any "politics". Our goal here is to present a Jewish understanding of the issue, in order to deepen dialogue, and to bring an additional details to a topic that creates so much passion. This is not a treatise about the values of Roe v. Wade or Dobbs v. Jackson. Rather it is a guide to help each individual deepen his or her understanding of traditional Jewish perspective, steeped in thousands of years of debate.

Source of Opinions

It is extremely important to understand that the translations used in this document are direct Hebrew to English translations; not based on the multiple interpretations through translation of the Septuagint[1]. We are looking at direct translations without any filter of various other multiple languages, and as such, these quotes are much clearer (and often different) than what many English text King James, NSV, or equivalent bibles say.

But these are the original texts that we are reviewing, and are accepted universally among academics, scholars, and theologians as being more accurate (which will ultimately only serve to empower our understandings further); as well as the translations that Jews have traditionally studied (if they are unable to directly translate the Hebrew themselves).

Opinions and Arguments

There is a long ago quip that two Jews equals three opinions, four Rabbis, and five synagogues. Jews have always engaged in dialogue and debates on any issue; and abortion is no different.

Since there are Torah and biblical instructions about how a pregnant mother, fetus, and the death of the fetus are to be treated, there have been debates about abortion practices going back to the earliest Rabbinic writings. We will track the development of the arguments regarding abortion and quote the ancient sources with citations to justify the legitimacy.

In Judaism, the strength of an argument is based on the text and its commentator's level of respect or acceptance in the Jewish world.

In order of importance, and therefore validity. Judaism places the words of Torah above all, followed by the text of the rest of the Bible—the Prophets and the Writings.

The accepted interpretation of those texts for over two thousand years is the Talmud (also known as the Oral Torah), and so the Talmud (composed structurally of the Mishna and Gemarra) is considered the primary source for understanding any religious law or practice from the Bible.

The great middle-age commentators such as Maimonides[2], Nachmonides[3], Rashi[4], and Tur[5] are placed on the next level of understanding, followed by commentators from the 16th-19th century who were great local Rabbis, who lived mostly in Europe. Least accepted are the commentaries by 20th and 21st century Rabbis. Although their opinions are valid and accepted within their communities; they usually do not have the gravitas or universal acceptance of Talmud or even medieval commentators.

For clarity's sake, we will try to focus as much as possible on the older and universally respected sources. This does not mean that in the 21st century an individual will accept them (think of how many Jews eat shellfish even though it is forbidden in the Torah); but it demonstrates that the Jewish philosophy is clear and not based on just personal feelings.

It is hoped that through an honest exploration of the texts and dialogues about abortion over the last two thousand years, a deeper understanding will be achieved of the real issues. But after going through this journey of exploration, it is vitally important that we remember to respect anyone who disagrees with our personal conclusions: on this or any other issue. Peace can only be achieved through respectful dialogue, and not by vitriol, violence, or hate towards a person with whom we disagree.

While intelligent people can disagree on how abortion should be viewed, it is more important that we respect each other in the midst of our passions. We may think someone is "wrong", but we should never view them as "evil" because they disagree with us.

Elu v'elu. These words and these words both have legitimacy and are words of the living God. May these words that follow present the brilliance of understanding found in the Sages of old, giving us all guidance and comfort in these challenging times.

Notes

1. 3rd century Greek translation of the Hebrew Bible, that was then used as the basis for translations into other languages over the centuries.
2. 12th century Rabbi, considered by many the greatest scholar and Rabbi of the last thousand years.
3. 13th century Rabbi who lived in Spain.
4. Rabbi Shlomo Yitzhak, 11th century French commentator, considered one of the greatest in history.
5. Rabbi Jacob ben Asher, 13th/14th century.

1

Abortion in the Ancient World

The concept of terminating a pregnancy through external means, techniques, or medicines has existed since the first human births; and each faith tradition and culture has had their own philosophical and legal opinions on the issue. In order to grasp the modern Jewish understanding of abortion, we need to briefly look at some of the beliefs and practices older cultures.

Although rarely referenced in the modern world, ancient Judaism had a "demon of abortion."

While never accepted in normative Judaism, there has been a folk belief for at least 2000 years that Adam, the first man, had a "first Eve[1]" who turned out not to be a suitable wife for Adam and was supplanted by the Eve that we meet in the first chapters of Genesis.

This earlier character called Lilith has developed

Do not destroy the children of Israel... As that Lilith, who, when she finds nothing else, turns upon her own children."

---

quite a following over the years, which persists in different forms even today[1]. Mentioned only once—in passing—in the Bible[3], this character of Lilith is brought up in the Talmud and also in later commentaries[4] as a being that seeks to destroy children.

One of the commentaries from Midrash Rabbah[5] is an exposition of the biblical story where Moses pleads with God to not destroy the Hebrew people[6], identifying Lilith as a being that destroys her own children:

In the Testament of Solomon,[7] it is claimed that Lilith moves about at night, visiting pregnant women and attempting to strangle their babies. The *Zohar*, the Jewish mystical text, also repeatedly alludes to one of her two purposes being to "strangle children"[8].

This idea of Lilith being a demon who causes the death of children in the womb and up until the eighth day after birth is continued throughout Rabbinic literature. This becomes the foundation for her still being the symbol of abortion activists.

James Joyce calls her the "patron saint of abortions"[9] But Lilith is only one of the ways ancient cultures explained or justified abortion.

While the practice of abortion is debated throughout the ancient world, it seems that only in Assyrian law was it considered a capital crime punishable by death.[10]

Whereas the ancient Jewish culture might lay the blame of the choice of abortion on Lilith (rather

Lilith as depicted as the serpent by Michelangelo in the Sistine Chapel

than being self-inflicted, induced by a doctor, or done by what might be called a doula or midwife today or perhaps some other outside source). Other cultures wrestled with the practicalities of abortion in different ways.

Herbal practices for inducing an abortion were common throughout the ancient world, even though most cultures considered it a crime to abort a fetus. By aborting through the use of herbs, practices such as sitting over a steaming pot of water, or other intentional injury, it was then difficult to accuse a person or allege a crime since there was no proof of the intention to abort.

It is in the Greco-Roman world that we see therapeutic measures such as procedures by midwives to cause an abortion,[11] which include everything from herbs to physical exercises to creating surgical instruments to dilate the cervix and curette the uterus.

Second century Christan theologian, Tertullian describes the surgical tools needed for a dilation and evacuation.[12]

But even though it was Hippocrates who is credited with developing the tools for abortion through surgery, his original Oath (that all doctors swear to practice) once actually included a line specifically forbidding abortion through surgical practices. "I will not give a woman a pessary to cause abortion."[13]

Aristotle, who believed that there was no human soul present in a fetus until 40 days for a male and 90 days for a female, felt that abortion after those respective periods was "incompatible with holiness."[14]

The Greeks has developed the medicinal techniques to carry out an abortion, but simultaneously restricted or prohibited the procedure.

This was the ancient world within which Judaism formed its early understandings and opinions around abortion. In the two thousand years of development leading up to the 20th and 21st century legal decisions in the U.S Supreme Court of *Roe v. Wade* and *Dobbs v. Jackson* Women's Health Organization, nearly every culture, faith, and nation has developed their own laws and practices regarding abortion ranging from forbidden as a capital crime to entirely permitted with *no restrictions. But from a traditional* point of view, these practices and viewpoints of the last two millennia are inconsequential, and it is important to understand this reality before we delve more deeply into the Jewish understanding of the topic.

Since the first century with the destruction of the Second Temple in Jerusalem, Jews have largely, but not completely, existed in "the Diaspora," or outside of their own land of Israel.

At the same time that Jews usually desired to be integrated into living side by side with other cultures — a life often denied to them — they, as a people, have strived to keep their authentic Jewish identity.

Assimilation, long thought to be a positive concept in American society, has always been accepted as a danger, one that has the potential to dissolve the Jewish people.

Despite what others around them may eat, Jews observed the laws of kashrut, that is kept kosher and observed holidays like Yom Kippur and Pesach (Passover) . While their Christian neighbors celebrated Christmas and and Easter, observing the Sabbath on Sundays, Jews do not recognize Jesus as the Messiah and keep the Sabbath from Friday eve until Saturday night.

Even though staying true to Jewish theology often led to persecutions around the world for two thousand years, the traditional Jewish belief is to never let go of Jewish teachings and practices in favor of assimilating.

It is easy for the modern Jew to assimilate, take on the practices and philosophies of gentiles, and ignore or even reject their Jewish faith and laws. This is especially true in America. But the fact that individuals, or even large groups of Jews, choose to embrace different viewpoints does not change actual Jewish practices, dialogues, laws, and understandings in relation to any issue, including abortion.

We must embrace the practice of "elu v'elu," but the words and concepts of the debate must be ensconced in Jewish text and understandings; not as a result of an blanket acceptance of another people's beliefs.

It is for this reason that we will stay focused in the Jewish arguments and understandings rather than incorporate the philosophies of other cultures, faiths, or modern secularism into our exploration of the

Jewish perspective on abortion. It is important to see how some of the opinions of the ancient cultures might have influenced early Jewish development (Greco-Roman and Assyrian for example). However, by the 3rd century Judaism had already developed its own unique pathway. It is this distinctiveness that we will explore more deeply.

A Hasidic tale relates how a rabbi went to a village and saw a lot of targets with arrows in the direct center bull's eye. He asked who the great archer was, and was told that it was Moshe, only nine years old. He went to Moshe and asked him if he was indeed the expert marksman. The boy replied that yes, it was he. The Rabbi asked him how he became so accurate. "It's easy," the boy replied. "I shoot the arrow first and then draw the target around it."

For the assimilated Jew who has adopted a personal and even passionate belief in pro-life or pro-choice, it is all too often like the little boy, Moshe. They have decided that they have their belief (usually adopted from others), and then try to back Jewish theology into their belief structure.

Similarly, many non-Jews hear of read something about Jewish belief and accept that it is true, exploring no further.

We need to investigate the actual beliefs, sources, texts, and understandings of the issue from an authentic Jewish perspective instead of trying to place Judaism into our own personal box. Judaism, as we will see, has a rich and complex history and understanding on abortion, and it is this that we will now explore more fully.

Notes

1. Known as "Chava ha'Rishona" referred to in Bereshit Rabbah 22:7 and again in Bamidbar Rabbah 16:25, this is the character that is usually referred to as "Lilith"

2. Founded in 1976, Lilith Magazine is a Jewish feminist magazine publishing quarterly; and The Lilith Fund, founded in 2001 is the oldest abortion fund in Texas as examples.

3. Isaiah 34:124

4. 1st century B.C.E Dead Sea Scrolls; 9th century Alphabet of Ben Sira; 10th century Midrash Abkir; and the Zohar of the 13th century to name a few

5. Bamidbar Rabbah 16:25, 12th century

6.Exodus 32:10

7. A Greek text attributed to the 1st century, but probably written pseudopigraphically in the Middle Ages

8. Zohar i 14b, 54b; ii 95a, 111a, to name a few

9. *Ulysses* Episode 14, "Oxen of the Sun"

10. Code os Assura, 1075 B.C.E

11. Plato's Theaetetus refers to midwives performing a gynecological procedure

12 Tertullian (1885) [c. 203]. "Tertullian Refutes, Physiologically, the Notion that the Soul is Introduced After Birth". A Treatise on the Soul. in Philip Schaff. Ante-Nicene Fathers. 3. Edinburgh: T&T Clark.

13. The Oath is from the Hippocratic Corpus, and this line is in the third paragraph of the Oath.

14. Politic vii16

2

The Sanctity of Life in Judaism

Throughout history, few traditions of the world, if any, have placed the sanctity of physical life on a greater level of importance than Judaism. When the majority of the world was still practicing human sacrifices, Judaism was committed to avoid the practices of Moloch, who sacrificed children.[1] Humanity is made in the image of God[2], and as such the Divine image should never be defiled or damaged. The prohibition on murder is expressed multiple times, most especially in the Ten Commandments.[3]

Judaism takes this sanctity outside of just developed human life and even into the animal kingdom, forbidding the cruel treatment of an animal[4] or the eating of its blood[5]. Physical life is a gift from God, and humans are forbidden from destroying that Divine gift. This biblical understanding is amplified through the many books of the Talmud. Here, the ancient Sages expressly forbid the taking of even one life. This was not merely based upon the Biblical prohibition against murder, but rather because of the potential that could come from that one life.

The value of human life is paramount in Judaism. Even the most stringent laws are to be

"Therefore, Adam the first man was created alone, to teach you that with regard to anyone who destroys one soul from the Jewish people, i.e., kills one Jew, the verse ascribes him blame as if he destroyed an entire world, as Adam was one person, from whom the population of an entire world came forth. And conversely, anyone who sustains one soul from the Jewish people, the verse ascribes him credit as if he sustained an entire world."

broken if it will save a life[6]. But it is important to remember that this prohibition is not only because of the destruction of the Divine Image, but also because of the destruction of a potential future. This becomes germane to our discussion about abortion as it is the argument of the Sages that it is criminal to destroy potential lives. Even if a proponent of abortion does not consider the destruction of the fetus a crime because of the fetus being "alive" (one of the many arguments of those against abortion: that the fetus is "alive" and to abort equates to murder); our Sages enjoin us to consider the potential future as well. If a baby ultimately is born, then we are to remember that the future progeny of that child is in themselves "an entire world" (ibid.)

Because the human body is created in the Divine image, desecrating the body through tattoos, piercing, and self-mutilation are also prohibited. The Torah is clear:

"You shall not make gashes on your flesh for the dead, or incise any marks upon yourselves."[7]

"One who imprints a tattoo is liable to lashes."[8]

Tosafot[9] expressly forbid any form of tattooing or piercing.

Obligation to Pro-Create:

The primary command given by God to human beings is "Be fruitful, and multiply". There is a common misperception that this commandment is the first to be given to humans; but Rashi, Nachmanides as well as Tosafot[10] on the this biblical passage[11] agree that this verse in Genesis 1:28 is a blessing that is analogous to the blessing of animals. The commandment version to "Be fruitful and multiply and replenish the earth" is found in Genesis 9:1.[12] This commandment is so important that the Sages teach that to not do this is "as if he has committed murder" and "as if he diminished the Divine image".[13]

Moreover, we are taught, "...when a man is brought to Judgment, he is asked: Did you deal fairly in commerce? Did you have fixed time for learning (the sacred texts of religion)? Did you undertake to fulfill the duty of pro-creation?"[14] Clearly pro-creation is extremely important in Judaism.

But it is equally important to understand that Judaism does not view sexuality as only for pro-creation. "If he takes for himself another wife; her food, her garment, and her duty of marriage, shall he not diminish"[15] is constantly interpreted by our Sages as meaning that it is a man's duty to sexually pleasure his wife as a duty of marriage. In Judaism, while there is a commandment for pro-creation, there is also an obligation commandment for pleasure within marriage; and so no argument can be devised against or pro accepting of abortion based on human sexuality being used only for the purpose of children.

It is useful for us to recognize the power of this commandment to the sons of Noah in detail, and how it is interpreted in Judaism. The command to "be fruitful and multiply" is given to Noah and his sons; and that is repeated specifically to Jacob later on[16], is directed to specific people on behalf of all humanity. Because the majority of the ancient Sages consider the command to being given to men, they state "The man is required to be fruitful and multiply, but not the woman"[17]. The Talmud teaches that "a man must have children", and discuss whether it can be at least two boys or a boy and a girl[18] as a fulfillment of that obligation. Although there are some minority opinions, the general consensus among our Sages and teachings is that the command to pro-create is an obligation for men only. Women are not obligated to have children[19].

This understanding cannot be overstated, as it is a foundation stone that demonstrates the value of women's rights in Judaism. Women are not obligated to have children, while men are. This dialogue is continued throughout the Talmud and other commentaries to discuss how men cannot use certain methods of birth control, but women also can use contraceptive techniques[20].

While this is different from current Catholic theology, it is a philosophical and theological base that demonstrates a primary Jewish truth: In much Jewish theology and practice, the majority of rights are with the woman. This ultimately means that the issue of abortion, from a Jewish perspective, is about a woman's rights and responsibilities[21].

The Rights of the Mother

Judaism gives rights to nearly everyone and everything, including animals and plants, but the primary rights are given to humanity[22]. With these rights come responsibilities. In the Torah, humans are given "dominion" over the animals, not "domination."[23] We are commanded to take care of the world,[24] and of each other.

A mother has special rights and responsibilities. The Holy Zohar[25] teaches that the tears of a mother open all the gates of heaven[26]. The importance of a "mother" is found in the deepest of kabbalistic teachings ranging from the foundational importance of the "mothers" in the Hebrew alphabet[27] to the understanding of the energy center of wisdom being called a "mother"[28].

"Chava," the Hebrew name of "Eve" in the Book of Genesis, translates to "mother of the world", and the very presence of God in the physical world is known as the Shechinah, which again is feminine in nature. Each week, Jews are reminded to honor the feminine as we welcome the "Sabbath Bride"[29] into our homes and hearts.

While a woman is not obligated to observe the commandments of the Torah with the same rigor as a man, she is given all the same rights, and even more so. Respect for women is so primary and clear in Jewish teachings that nearly all sacred objects in Judaism are feminine in their word structure[30]. Mezuzah[31], Shabbat[32], Havdalah[33], and even Torah are all feminine words. Given all these factors, especially that women are even exempt from observance of many of the 613 Torah commandments, it is clear that respect for women and honoring them in every way is a fundamental piece of traditional Jewish thought and practices[34].

Legal Status of the Fetus:

The traditional set of laws regarding abortion begin with the legal status of the fetus. The Talmud has a clear phrase, "The fetus is regarded as one of the limbs of the mother"[35]. This becomes a primary piece of text for understanding Jewish law regarding abortion, and so must be explained a bit.

"The fetus is regarded as one of the limbs of the mother"

There are multiple proof texts for this concept that the fetus is part of the mother in cases much less important than abortion. If an animal is bought, and then found to be pregnant, the future animal belongs to the new owner.[36]

In the matter of conversion, a pregnant convert does not have to have her child go through the process again after birth, but is considered a recipient of the mother's choices. A fetus has no rights of acquisition, and cannot receive a gift or transaction by anyone other than its father.

There is clearly no legal standing on the part of the fetus according to the Sages, who in multiple dialogues even go so far as to say that a baby does not have the same legal standing as a fully living being.

In the case of a still unborn child, the laws of mourning do not apply, and feticide is distinguished from homicide or infanticide. This even stems from the Bible itself: "If men quarrel, and hurt a pregnant woman, so that her fruit depart from her, and yet no further harm befalls [her]; he shall be surely punished, according to what the woman's husband will lay upon him; and he shall pay as the judges etermine. But if further harm befall her, then thou shall give life for life".

Death of the fetus is a tort charge, punishable by monetary relief; whereas death to the mother is a capital crime. While the fetus is not on the same legal level as the mother (and does not require capital punishment), this text does make it clear however that it cannot and

> *"If men quarrel, and hurt a pregnant woman, so that her fruit depart from her, and yet no further harm befalls (her); he shall be surely punished, according to what the woman's husband will lay upon him; and he shall pay as the judges determine.*

should not be injured in any way; and that to do so is criminal. But the fetus itself has no legal rights and is considered part of the mother.

At first glance, it might seem that since the fetus has no legal rights, abortion would be allowed in any instance. But Jewish practices are based on deeper analysis of words, phrases, concepts, and texts, as well as will integrate ethical understandings of potential of life that we will explore momentarily. But first, we need to examine the statement from Exodus a bit more from purely a legal standpoint.

Based on Exodus 21:22 it is clear that injuring the fetus is criminal, but not on a capital crime level. The criminality of it is because it hurts the mother, as well as the potential for life. But it is not capital as the fetus is not a human being in the legal sense. The Exodus statement is clearly using the example of an outside person hurting the fetus, but what if the woman decides to hurt the fetus herself?

Maimonides and the *Shulchan Arukh*[37] maintain that a person has no right to inflict damage even upon themself[38], and so many authorities throughout the ages have been clear that abortion by choice is forbidden because it is equivalent to hurting oneself. As discussed earlier, any act that desecrates the human body is forbidden. If this applies to tattoos, self-mutilation, etc., how much more so does it apply when there is a combination of hurting oneself and destroying the potential for human life? And this does not yet deal with the reasons to prohibit abortion on other ethical grounds of threatening that potential life.

As we saw earlier, the potential future is integrated into the reasons to prohibit murder. The death of fetus is also the death of all future generations that could ultimately come as a result of that child growing into a parent themselves. Jewish tradition is clear that this potential future must be considered in all of our acts. One of the more commonly repeated values of Judaism is "l'dor v'dor": from generation to generation. We are to look not only at what our actions do in the present, but how they might affect the future.

Since we are the ones who are to take care of this physical world, it is our obligation to make sure that life is always sustained and enhanced. Based on this understanding, it is clear that to eliminate the potential for life unnecessarily is a violation of Jewish ethics. In the same way that we would not (without clear reasoning) destroy seeds that could become plants, we are prohibited from destroying any potential for life. Even in cases of war, we are prohibited from the practice of rampant destruction including any sort of vandalism[39], and are especially prohibited from destroying any living thing such as a plant, tree, or animal[40]. Life, whether actualized or potential, is to be treasured at all times.

The 17th century Turkish scholar, Rabbi Joseph *Trani additionally makes the clear argument* based on the Talmudic passages in Yevamot 63b that the issue of abortion is tort and not capital; but that it is criminal as it "diminishes God's image" (as the Talmud says with regard to neglecting the duty or pro-creation). From the legal perspective we have studied so far, we know abortion is criminal (as a tort) because of how it hurts the woman and how it diminishes God's image.

From this Jewish legal perspective, abortion is criminal without basing the argument on anything to do with the fetus' rights.[41]

Notes

1. Leviticus 20:1-5
2. Genesis 1:26
3. Exodus 20:13 and Deut 5:17
4. Exodus 20:10, 23:5, Leviticus 22:28, Deuteronomy 23:25, 25:4 to name a few
5. Leviticus 17:13
6. Called "pikuach nefesh", saving a life is the highest priority in Judaism. The only commandments that cannot be broken to save a life are adultery, idolatry, and committing murder according to Maimonides.
7. . Leviticus 19:29
8. Mishnah Makkot 3:6
9. Bavli Gittin 20b
10. Middle Age commentators that were included as part of the Talmud
11. Babylonian Talmud, Yevamot 63b
12. This may seem like a meaningless distinction, but our Sages are clear, and we will see shortly, why it is so important to realize that 1:28 is a blessing and 9:1 is a commandment
13. Babylonian Talmud, Yevamot 63b
14. Babylonian Talmud, Shabbat 31a
15. Exodus 21:10
16. Genesis 35:11
17. Mishna Yevamot 6:6. The concept is expounded in Rabbinic dialogue in Babylonian Talmud Yevamot 65b
18. Ibid.
19. This also makes common sense when considering how difficult and risky pregnancy and childbirth can be; and allows the woman the opportunity to not take that risk

20. Talmud makes specific references to contraceptive teas; an item which is similar to a modern diaphragm; a post coital contraceptive tea and ointment, among other things. This topic is deeply delved into, especially in the Talmudic tractates Yevamot and Ketuvot.

21. This is important as it changes the entire nature of the "pro-life/pro-chioce" debate; and gives women a sense of empowerment as opposed to degradation (often the feeling that is expressed when they are told that the fetus is as important as they are).

22. Genesis 1:28, 9:2

23. Ibid.

24. Genesis 2:15

25. Foundational work of Jewish mystical thought. Traditionally attributed to R. Shimon Bar Yochai in the 2nd century, although possibly written pseudo-picagraphically by Moses de Leon in the 13th century

26. Zohar, Shemot 22

27. Sefer Bahir, 1st century Book of Mystical teachings

28. Ibid.

29. The archetype of feminine energy and personification of the spirit of the Sabbath

30. Like many other languages, Hebrew conjugates words in both masculine and feminine

31. The box containing a scroll with biblical commandments found on the doors in Jewish homes

32. The Sabbath

33. The first act in the physical world that God performs, and the name of the ceremony observed at the end of each Sabbath

34. Sadly, today there are many misogynistic practices found in some Jewish communities. But this is a direct

result of assimilating Catholic practices in the Middle Ages in Europe, and are not part of Jewish thought.

35. Babylonian Talmud, Gittin 23b; again referenced in Chullin 58b

36. Babylonian Talmud, Bava Kama 78a

37. Code of Jewish Law from the 16th century that is considered the authoritative resource of "how" to practice laws and observe commandments

38. Yad, Hovel U-Mazzik 5, 1, and Sh. Ar H.M. 424, after Babylonian Talmud Bava Kamma 90b

39. Rabbi Norman Lamm Bal Tashhit: The Torah Prohibits Wasteful Destruction

40. ibid.

41. Babylonian Talmud 89b discusses how the embiyo is not formed into a fetus until the 40th day; but the argument that we posited earlier is not based on the fetus' rights; and so it becomes inconsequential whether the embryo is in the first trimester or third.....all of it is considered a tort crime and punishable by monetary damages. This is a much stronger argument than being based on "the soul entering at conception" from a Jewish perspective.

3

When is the fetus a "human being"?

Many statements have been made on when a fetus is considered "human".

"From the time that the ovum is fertilized, a new life is begun which is neither that of the father nor of the mother; it is rather the life of a new human being with his own growth. It would never be made human if it were not human already." (Catholic Doctrine from Congregation for the Doctrine of Faith, 1974)

"The Catholic Church teaches and has taught that life—human life—begins at conception." (Cardinal Wilton Gregory, 2021)

"The Bible teaches that human beings are made in the image and likeness of God (Genesis 1:27, 9:6) and protectable human life begins at fertilization." (Southern Baptist Convention, 1999, Resolution 7)

"The soul or spirit of the individual comes into being with the conception of his physical body." (Bahai Faith, Lights of Guidance #1699, 10/9/1947)

"Antoninus also said to Rabbi, When is the soul placed in man; as soon as it is decreed [that the sperm shall be male or female, etc.], or when [the embryo] is actually formed? He replied, From the moment of formation. He objected: Can a piece of meat be unsalted for three days without becoming putrid? But it must be from the moment that [God] decrees [its destiny]. Rabbi said: This thing Antoninus taught me, and Scripture supports him, for it is written, And thy decree hath preserved my spirit [i.e., my soul]." (Bavli, Sanhedrin 91b)

"I feel that for the formation of life, for something to actually become a human, something more is needed than simply a fertilized egg." (Dalai Lama, 10th Mind and Life Institute Conference, 2003)

There is an old joke that three clergy were asked when a fetus becomes a full human being. The Priest said at the moment of conception, the Minister replied at the moment of birth, and the Rabbi said when the child graduates medical school. A silly statement, but on a different level it reflects the vast opinions of this primary question: when does the fetus have a soul and is a human being?

Judaism has a concept known as "secrets of God". This is an understanding that while we can explore certain issues around birth, life, death, the cosmos, etc., but we can never really _know_ the truth for certain as they are secrets of God.

One of these secrets is "ensoulment". At what point does the soul enter? There is a lot of discussion and varied opinions on it among the Sages and texts — ranging from at the moment of conception to when the crown of the head of the baby is visible — but we accept that this is truly a mystery that we cannot ever know for sure, as it is one of God's secrets.

It is the topic of ensoulment that leads to many of the most passionate spiritual arguments on both sides of the abortion issue.

Although it is now the accepted Catholic dogma, ensoulment at conception was not part of Church doctrine until the influence of the Pythagorean Greek movement in the third century by Father Tertullian, confirmed by St. Gregory of Nysa in the 4th century, and accepted by Augustine in the 5th century. Even in the 6th century, the famed Justinian Code exempted abortions before 40 days from punishment. While the Church now accepts that ensoulment happens at conception, this was not Catholic theology for many of the early centuries of Catholicism.

Judaism has many discussions on the topic. While Judaism accepts that the soul exists before the physical birth[1], there are many propositions as to when the soul enters the fetus.

Rabbi Yehuda HaNasi, the redactor of the Mishnah, expresses that it is from the moment of formation. "[2]Elsewhere in the Talmud, we find two of the greatest Sages, Rabbi Eliazar and Rabbi Yohanan agreeing that the soul enters the fetus on the fortieth day, based on the concept that Torah was given in forty days[3].

This dialogue continues until today, with Rabbis throughout the centuries arguing for ensoulment at conception[4], at forty days, at sixty days, and at the moment that labor begins. But because the definitive answer is a "secret of God", we do not base our laws on what cannot be known. Therefore, from a Jewish perspective, while there are ethical considerations with a fetus being aborted, we base the law on the basis that ensoulment has occurred by the time when either the crown of the head of the baby has been revealed or at 36 weeks (since it is accepted that at 36 weeks the baby is fully developed and viable). At either of those times, the fetus is considered its own life and has the rights of a living being with a soul. Prior to that, Jewish law does not consider the fetus an entity of its own with its own rights, but a limb of the mother.

Because of the question of ensoulment, and the lesser legal status of the fetus, the mother's life always takes precedence over the fetus. But at what point does that change?

Again, our Sages were clear, "If a woman has life threatening difficulty with childbirth, one dismembers the embryo she carries because her life takes precedence over its life. Once its head (or its "greater part") has emerged, it may not be touched, for we do not set aside one life for another"[5].

This is explained in more detail with the concept of a "rodef," a pursuer.

Notes

1. Jeremiah 1:5 is clear that God knew the soul of Jeremiah before the fetus was formed in his mother's belly

2. Babylonian Talmud, Sanhedrin 91b

3. Babylonian Talmud, Menachot 99b

4. There is even a kabbalistic concept expressed in Margaliyot HaYam that every time a couple make love properly, it metaphysically results in a soul being born which, even if it does not come to fruition, exists and will take physical form when the Messiah comes

5. Mishnah, Oholot 7,6; paralleled in Babylonian Talmud Sanhedrin 72b

4

The Pursuer

*R*odef is a Hebrew term meaning "pursuer", and is used legally throughout the Talmud to describe someone who is pursuing a potential victim to kill them[1]. If you see a rodef, you are allowed to stop him by whatever means necessary from fulfilling his task. "According to the law, you deserve to be slain, since you are a pursuer, and the Torah has said, If one comes to kill your rise and kill him first."[2]

This becomes the term used throughout the Talmud and our commentaries to describe a fetus and the relation to the mother in terms of whether abortion should be permitted.

Simply put, if the fetus is a rodef, pursuing the mother's life, there is little question about whether abortion is permitted. The fetus has no legal status as we have seen. As a result, the mother's life is more important than the potential fetus' life (based on the secret of not really knowing ensoulment). Once the fetus has a legal status (by the crown or greater part of the baby being exposed, or by the completion of 36 weeks of pregnancy according to other Talmudic texts), we do

> *"For only a pursuer may be killed in self-defense of for defense of another, but this fetus is not pursuer… We must save her by other treatments:"*

not sacrifice the soul of one being for another… and so the mother is not allowed to have an abortion even if the baby is putting the mother's life at risk. At that point, the Sages ask the question as to whether the baby is actually the rodef to the mother or is the mother a rodef to the baby[3]. Since we cannot determine which; at that point, abortion is forbidden even if the mother's life is at risk. "For only a pursuer may be killed in self defense of for defense of another, but this fetus is not pursuer… We must save her by other treatments:"[4]

We see that abortion is permitted if the mother's life is in danger, assuming that the fetus does not have legal status based on 36 weeks or revealing of crown or greater part. Other than those circumstances, it is seemingly forbidden based on early Jewish texts. But we must remember that the woman's rights are paramount throughout Judaism, and this is where we start to get a different argument for other types of abortion than "therapeutic abortion".

The Rabbis argue repeatedly about the influence and importance of "mental health". We know that psychological or emotional health is an important part of physical health, but is it substantial enough to potentially diminish the Divine image?

This is the formation of the arguments used in the 20th century by liberal rabbinic sources to justify abortion. The fetus is considered by those favoring the use of abortions (that are other than therapeutic) is that the fetus is a rodef...pursuing the psycho-emotional wellbeing of the mother and as such, endangering her life physically.

This is a valid argument and must be appreciated as such. There are cases where the baby could potentially be such a painful experience (i.e. caused by rape or incest) that the mother considers thoughts of suicide rather than having the baby. In this case, where the mother is truly suicidal, the fetus is clearly a rodef. But that is very different than the mother just being uncomfortable with the fetus or finds pregnancy undesirable.

The Jewish View of Abortion

Remember that the fetus is considered a limb of the mother: this is *all* about women's rights (and the responsibilities that go along with those rights) and not rights of the fetus. The fetus, as a "limb" of the mother, does not have rights. But the mother has the responsibility of taking good care of her body, whether it is the "limb" of a fetus or the limb of an arm. In the same way that Judaism does not allow you to cut off your arm because of a scratch (although you might have to amputate because of a severe injury or sickness in order to live), Judaism strictly forbids aborting a fetus because it is inconvenient.

Understanding this basic principle, in conjunction with the legal status of the fetus, makes it clear that ethically it is extreme to abort a fetus unless there is real, clear, and defined risk to the mother's life. In answer to those who would ask how you can tell if a woman's life is at risk, even psycho-emotionally, it might be useful to demonstrate the concept with a non-abortion analogy.

If a man comes into the hospital with a cut arm and is in such pain that he wants to amputate, the doctors know that the arm will be fine with a few antibiotics and a bandage. What should be done? Should the arm be amputated because the man in that moment is in pain? Should the rest of his life, as well as the lives of everyone around him who can be positively influenced by what he can do with his arm, be destroyed and cut off because of only thinking of the momentary discomfort as opposed to the full length of his days? In the future, would that man have a legitimate lawsuit against that doctor who amputated because the doctor did not do his duty and save the arm, even though the man was screaming to just cut it off?

If this circumstance actually happened in a hospital, it is doubtful that there is a doctor in the nation who would needlessly amputate the arm. If he did, the patient would be examined for mental illness, and the doctor would probably lose his license to practice medicine. Conversely, if the man had been a musician, and the injury sustained would clearly prevent him from ever playing his instrument again, it might ultimately be a different story. If he is unquestionably clear[5] that he would commit suicide rather than suffer the reminder of what he once was by looking at the arm, there might be a legitimate argument that some doctors would make to amputate (however, very few doctors would be likely to consider amputation even in that extreme circumstance).

Using this analogy, it becomes clear how abortion that is not based on a life risk to the mother is

> *"It is a poverty to decide that a child must die so that you may live as you wish." - Mother Teresa*

inappropriate. Combined with this is the obligation (for both men and women) to not diminish the Divine image. By pointlessly amputating an arm, or by needlessly aborting, the Divine image is being diminished as a limb is being removed. Only in the case of a clear threat to the mother's life does it make sense ethically (as we have previously established)…not because of the potential ensoulment of the fetus, but because it diminishes the Divine image and is needless.

Notes

1. The term "pursuer" first appears in the Bible in the Book of Proverbs 19:7, in which the concept is tied to someone who bears false witness. The term is extended in the Talmud and Rabbinic literature to describe a person who "pursues another with the intention of killing him" as described by the Sages in Bava Kama, Berachot, and Sanhedrin to name a few of the tractates.

2. Babylonian Talmud, Berachot 62b

3. Per Babylonian Talmud, Sanhedrin 72b, the mother is at that point being "pursued by heaven".

4. Pahad Yitzhak; R. Isaac Lampronti 18th century

5. The standards are similar to those required by most states for a 5150 involuntary psychiatric hold: the person must be identified as being a danger to himself and/or others, and must have the means to accomplish their goal. Similarly, the patient would need to be psycho/spiritually examined to determine whether they were truly going to commit suicide

5

What about dad, the family, and the world?

In the present personal narcissism that has infiltrated 21st century culture, it is easy to forget that more people are affected by the choice to abort a baby than just the mother and child. Shouldn't we also consider how the proposed abortion might affect other people? Since the grandparents, siblings, and especially the father of the baby will be affected by an abortion, shouldn't they have a say in this decision making?

The simple answer to this question is both yes and no. On the one hand, the halachic (legal) responsibility is entirely in the hands of the mother. From a Jewish legal perspective, it is her responsibility to only abort if the baby is a rodef, and ultimately her legal responsibility alone.

But here again we find that Judaism is not monolithic, and simultaneously embraces the opposites of elu v'elu.

There is a Jewish concept of *lifnei mishurat ha'din*, literally meaning "inside or before the line of the law". It is an ancient Jewish understanding that while the law can legislate what can and cannot be done; it is possible for a person to act "legally" and still act like a jerk to others. We have all known people like this: they follow the letter of the law exactly, but with no regard as to how their actions hurt other people. This idea of acting "inside" the law is a concept enacted so that people are kinder, more respectful, and more considerate of each other. It comes from the Talmudic understanding[1] of Deut. 6:18 that instructs that "you should do the straight and the good in the eyes of God…"

In many commentaries on the Talmud, most notably Ramban[2], this is understood to mean that this verse is teaching us that while we must keep God's specific laws, we must also institute what is "good and straight" in those areas for which God did not issue any specific rules. The laws cannot legislate for more than a fraction of the ethical dilemmas that we face in life. The idea is that even if something is not specifically prohibited in the Torah, we should still act in a way that is consonant with the ethics and values of authentic Judaism. As Rav Yosef Dov Soloveitchik taught, "Halacha (Jewish law) is a floor, not a ceiling".

One of the best examples I know of this practice of lifnei mishurat ha'din is a personal story that was shared with me by my friend and teacher, Rabbi Elijah Schochet. When Rabbi Schochet was a child, he was once walking with his father in Chicago. At a certain point, his father, who was also a great scholar and righteous man, slowed the young boy down. When they got home, his father asked him, "Eli, do you know

"Halacha is a floor, not a ceiling"

why we slowed down during our walk?" The young boy replied that he did not, and was educated by his father in what lifnei mishurat ha'din truly means. "Up ahead of us was an old man who was walking slowly. We didn't need to rush by and make him feel older and infirm. This is why we slowed down." This is the epitome of this primary Jewish concept: to act in ways that take into account the feelings and experiences of other people besides ourselves, and to make our decisions not just based on the law, but upon ethics and consideration.

And where does this concept of *lifnei mishurat ha'din* enter our discussion with regard to abortions?

There is a process known by different names that we will call "stakeholder analysis." It is used by many businesses and organizations and indeed some cultures when dealing with conflict resolution. It entails exploring who all the "stakeholders" are in a process before coming to a decision, and in this way creating a foundation for a decision that will be righteous for everyone.

Here, the halacha evaluates the primary stakeholders of the mother and child. But based on *lifnei mishurat ha'din*, we must also look at other stakeholders before deciding to support a mother's legal right to abort based on the laws we've discussed.

Although a potential father has no legal claim to determining whether to abort or not, he most certainly is dramatically affected by the decision. Remembering that the obligation to procreate is placed on the man, the mother's decision to abort may prohibit him from fulfilling that commandment. The various family members also are affected, as a new member of the family may be the exact blessing that some family members need for their souls. And the community is directly affected as well, especially in this 21st century world where so many couples are having fertility issues and over two million couples are desperately looking to adopt a baby in the United States alone.[3]

In Jewish law, the principle of lifnei mishurat ha'din must be considered with regard to these additional stakeholders before having the procedure of an abortion. Even though these people have no legal standing in the discussion and decision-making based on the clear understanding that this is about a mother's rights and responsibilities. On the other hand, their lives too are affected by the decision, and this concept of lifnei mishurat ha'din demands that the mother not make the decision unilaterally, but with the counsel and input of other stakeholders. Although it is ultimately her decision alone to make, the principle of lifnei mishurat ha'din guides her to not go through the decision-making process alone.

Additional Understanding of Jewish Theology:

Jewish law is very strict with Jews, but very lenient with non-Jews. The law that is most repeated in the Torah is to treat the stranger with respect (as we were once strangers in the strange land of Egypt). As an example, while Jews are commanded to follow the laws of Kashrut (what foods you can and cannot eat), there is no proscription placed on non-Jews. While we have 613 laws in the Torah that we are to follow, there are only 7 for non-Jews (called the Noahide laws[4]).

Similarly, while these laws and understandings are applicable for Jews, we would not enforce them upon non-Jews. This is an important understanding politically. In the same way that I don't eat shellfish but have no issue with the person eating it across from me, this concept makes it clear that it doesn't matter what a political candidate's personal view is on the issue of abortion and whether a fetus has a soul at conception or never has one. What matters is the rights and responsibilities of the mother, and it is this legal concept that forbids abortion except in the most extreme life-threatening cases. By taking the argument away from the rights of the fetus and shifting it towards the rights of the woman (as the Jewish argument against abortion does), it may be more acceptable to the person who does not believe that the fetus has a soul and is exclusively concerned with the "woman's body" to have a dialogue about abortion without vitriolic passion.

What about dad, the family, and the world?

Endnotes

1. Bava Metzia 30b
2. Aka Nachmanides, 13th century
3. www.americanadoptions.com
4. Identified in Babylonian Talmud, Sanhedrin 56 a/b, these
laws are: prohibitions against idol worship, cursing God,
murder, adultery/sexual immorality, theft, eating flesh of
a living animal, and a positive commandment to establish
courts of justice.

6

Secular Law vs. Jewish law

Jewish law is built upon ethical and spiritual streams integrated with practicality. Ultimately it is based upon a perceived understanding of God's intention as expressed in the Torah and subsequent commentaries.

But secular law is not based on those values, but on interpretations of the primary legal documents such as the U.S. Constitution through courts. While we are not here to examine the constitutional interpretations of the court decisions, it is important to see how the current laws regarding abortion (which are constantly changing) are in harmony or antithetical to Jewish laws on the topic. The most recent national legal decision was the U.S. Supreme Court decision on Dobbs vs Jackson in 2022.

Although this was condemned by abortion advocates as prohibiting abortion nationally, the text is actually very clear that this is an inaccurate understanding of the decision. This was a decision that only overruled *Roe vs Wade* and *Casey vs Planned Parenthood* of Southeastern Pa.[1] Those two cases had established that abortion was a constitutional right, and Dobbs merely stated that although abortion is not a constitutional right, neither is it forbidden constitutionally. Dobbs referred the "authority to regulate abortion returned to the people and their elected representatives". It neither protected, defined, nor prohibited the occular right to abortion. Despite the passions created over the last years about this decision, it actually has no bearing on the laws regarding abortion, rather making it a decision of elections and state legislation.

Roe vs Wade in 1973 however, which was overturned by Dobbs, radically affected abortion legalities. Its primary holding was that "a person has a right to an abortion until a fetus becomes viable... Viability means the ability to live outside the womb, which usually means between 24 and 28 weeks after conception."[2] To integrate this within Jewish law is actually not only meaningful, but has a result that may not mean what abortion advocates think...

There are three important aspects to Roe. The first is that all the rights until "viability" lie in the hands of the mother and not the fetus. As has been discussed, this is absolutely in harmony with Jewish law.

But the second aspect of Roe is about the responsibilities of the mother that we have explored in detail. Roe allows the mother to have rights but no responsibilities, which is antithetical to Jewish law and teachings. By having no personal responsibility, Roe allowed abortion to be used as a form of birth control for convenience: something clearly forbidden in Jewish law. This concept of giving a right without the accompanying responsibility is in direct opposition to the teachings of almost every spiritual tradition, especially Judaism, which seek to promote psycho-emotional maturity by integrating rights with responsibilities. In this respect, Roe undermines Jewish laws in general and the halacha regarding abortions specifically by not demanding any personal responsibility on the part of the mother. While the first aspect of all rights being with the mother is consonant with Jewish law, this second part is in opposition to the halacha.

The third aspect of the Roe decision is the most interesting, and actually affects Jewish law, although probably not in the way that abortion activists want or anticipate. This is the understanding of "viability" of the fetus.

Jewish law is clear that one life cannot be traded for another; and equally clear that an unviable fetus

57

has no rights. Based on this, our Sages established that while an abortion may take place if the fetus is a rodef, even that has limits. Jewish law is clear that the fetus is protected and cannot be aborted at either 36 weeks or when the crown of the baby's head was revealed. This was based on the ancient understanding of "viability", and that once the baby is viable to live on its own outside the womb, we do not trade one life for another. As discussed earlier, at the point of viability, determined as 36 weeks or the crown being revealed, we can no longer say who is the actual rodef: the mother or the baby.

The definition of viability was based on the medical practices of the time, so the marker was 36 weeks. But medical knowledge and practices have changed over the centuries. The amazing work done in Neo-Natal Intensive Care Units has allowed babies as young as 24 weeks to survive and ultimately thrive. This medical fact was codified in the Roe decision. Based on modern techniques, the definition of "viability" in Jewish law must be changed to be in harmony with secular medical knowledge.

Based on *Roe vs. Wade*, Jewish law must be redefined and updated in the same way that the prohibitions of creating fire on the Sabbath was updated in the 20th century to include turning on electricity. Judaism has a 2000-year-old history of changing legal definitions as new information or science dictate. As a result, Roe demands that an abortion because of a rodef is no longer forbidden after 36 weeks, but rather must be limited to 24 weeks.

As much as it may upset abortion activists, Jewish law (which is always adapting based in modern understandings) must integrate the Roe definition. The halacha is clear that given modern medical practices, abortion is forbidden entirely after 24 weeks, based on *Roe vs Wade*.

On a practical level, Dobbs changed the integration of Jewish and secular law in two ways. The first is to put the power of decision making about abortion laws back in the jurisdiction of each state. This has no real bearing on Jewish law per se; but forces us to look at state laws and compare each one to the halacha rather than a national law. The other change that Dobbs created, in conjunction with the understanding of "viability" as determined in Roe (and this definition was not contradicted in Dobbs) is that it establishes that no state law should, according to Jewish law, allow any sort of abortion past 24 weeks.

As of early 2024, this would mean that there would only be seven states that would be in direct violation of Jewish law[3] as they currently have no restrictions in abortion: Alaska, Colorado, District of Columbia, New Jersey, New Mexico, Oregon, Vermont. Since all other states either prohibit abortion entirely or until viability; the vast majority of the nation would fall within the

Jewish legal understanding. As of May, 2024[4], even the most stringent anti-abortion state laws allow abortions if the life of the mother is threatened, and so would be consonant with halachic understanding.

Integrating the viability decision of Roe vs Wade into a Jewish legal understanding, abortion is prohibited before 24 weeks unless it is life threatening to the mother, and entirely forbidden after 24 weeks.

With rights come responsibilities, and Judaism does not sacrifice any one life for another.

The Practical Concern of L'Dor V'Dor as a Good Deed for Others

While Judaism clearly posits a different understanding of the abortion issue than a simple "pro-life" vs. "pro-choice," there are two additional factors that Judaism considers: empathy and compassion, both for a future child and for potential parents.

We have discussed earlier how the potential for life in a fetus is magnified when we consider the many generations that may spring from that single life. By striving to let the fetus develop fully and be born, we are demonstrating compassion for both the present

With rights come responsibilities, and Judaism does not sacrifice any one life for another.

generation and future generations; this consciousness of future generational potentials is fundamental to Jewish practice.

Unless there is a danger to the mother's life, Jewish thought encourages the birth a single child to create the opportunity of future generations as an act of great compassion. It is the physical manifestation of "l'dor v'dor", as it allows for the creation of physical beings who will "praise God from generation to generation".

But choosing not to abort is also a great act of compassion for potential adoptive parents. If the birth parents are contemplating abortion because their lives are extremely difficult even without the baby, the option of placing the child up for adoption is considered a great mitzvah...a special good deed. The Talmud specifically states that an adopted child is to be treated as if the parents were the birth parents.[5] There are so many loving parents who are unable to physically have their own children, and could both gain and give so much by adopting.

Again, the words of Mother Teresa capture the sentiment that so many couples feel:

"Please don't kill the child. I want the child. Please give me the child. I am willing to accept any child who would be aborted, and to give that child to a married couple who will love the child, and be loved by the child. From our children's home in Calcutta alone, we have saved over 3,000 children from abortions. These children have brought such love and joy to their adopting parents, and have grown up so full of love and joy!"

Even if the fetus is considered an actual rodef on a psycho-emotional level, who would truly endanger the mother's future life, Judaism encourages us to try and fulfill this great mitzvah of adoption for the sake of l'dor v'dor...of future and present generations. Both children and couples can receive a great blessing rather than having a potential life aborted.

Notes

1. Casey vs Planned Parenthood was a Supreme Court decision in 1992 that strengthened Roe vs Wade by focusing on the 14th Amendment and individual rights. As a constitutional case based upon Roe, which was overturned in 2022, the Casey case has no bearing om the theological, philosophical, nor halachic aspects of our discussion.

2. https://supreme.justia.com/cases/federal/us/410/113/#:~:text=Pp.-,163%2C%20164.,or%20health%20of%20the%20mother.

3. https://aawellnessproject.org/3716-2/?gad_source=1

4. https://www.usnews.com/news/best-states/articles/a-guide-to-abortion-laws-by-state

5. Bavli, Sanhedrin 19B

Glossary

Bava Metzia: "the middle gate"; a tractate in the Talmud, much of which deals with commerce and business law

Bavli: Babylonian Talmud; central text of Rabbinic Judaism; composed of the Mishnah and Gemarrah; codified between 200-500 C.E.

Elu v'elu: "these and these"; the Jewish concept that contradictory statements may both be true

Gemara: Part of the Talmud; commentary and analysis of the Mishna

Halacha: Term applied to Jewish law as interpreted by the Talmud and later authoritiesHasid/Hasidic Movement

Havdalah: Literally, separation, referring to the ceremony and verbal declaration made at the end of Shabbat.

Hippocrates: An ancient Greek physician who lived during

65

Greece's Classical period and is traditionally regarded as the father of modern medicine. Said to have written the Hippocratic Oath, an ethical guide for conduct of the medical profession.

Justinian Code: A four-book collection of laws and legal interpretations developed under the sponsorship of the Byzantine emperor Justinian from 529-565 CE.

L'dor v'dor: A Hebrew phrase that means "from generation to generation."

Lifnei mishurat ha'din: The Jewish ideal is always to act beyond the letter of the law: lifnim mishurat hadin in Hebrew, literally means, inside the line of law.

Lilith: A female demon and consort of Satan or Samuel. According to one legend in Jewish tradition, she was Adams's first wife.

Machlochet: Constructive conflict, disagreeing without hate

Mezuzah: Literally, doorpost. The case contains a rolled parchment inscribed with several passages from Deuteronomy (6:4-9 and 11:13-21) affirming the unity of God. This case is attached to the right doorpost of the entrance doorway and of each room in Jewish homes.

Midrash Rabbah: (The Great Midrash) which consists of collections of midrashim on the Five Books of Moses and the Five Scrolls (Song of Songs, Ruth, Lamentations, Ecclesiastes, and Esther) written from the 6fth to 12th century CE.

Mishnah: First major collection of Jewish Oral Law and foundation of the Talmud; redacted by Yehuda ha'Nasi (Judah the Prince) in the second and third centuries

Glossary

Rabbi Eleazar: 1st century Mishnaic Sage and mystic

Rabbi Yehuda ha'Nasi: Also known as "Rav", 2nd century redactor of the Mishnah

Rabbi Yochanan: 1st century Mishnaic Sage and one of the primary contributors to the Mishnah

Rabbi Yosef Karo: 15th/16th century mystic and author of the *Shulchan Arukh*, a major source of Jewish law and practiced

Rabbi Yosef Soloveitchik: 20th century American Orthodox Jewish scholar and philosopher

Rambam: 12th century Rabbi, philosopher, commentator; Moses ben Maimon, also known as Maimonides; author of *Mishneh Torah*, a major Jewish legal code

Ramban: 13th century Rabbi, scholar, and mystic Moses ben Nachman, also known as Nachmanides

Rashi: Rabbi Shlomo Yitzhaki; 11th century French Rabbi and prolific Torah and Talmud commentator

Rodef: a pursuer with an intent to harm or kill

Sanhedrin: Tractate in the Talmud that often deals with the world to come as well as deep religious or mystical philosophy

Septuagint: Greek translation of the Hebrew Bible from the 3rd century B.C.E.; by tradition based on the translatioms of 72 Hebrew translators

Shabbat: Jewish Sabbath; begins on Friday at sunset and ends on Saturday night

Shulchan Arukh: "Set Table;" a code of Jewish law written in the 16th century by Rabbi Yosef Karo

Talmud: Central Text of Rabbinic Judaism composed of Mishneh and Gemara; two slightly different versions edited in Babylon (Bavli).and Jerusalem (Yerushalmi)

Tertullian: 2nd century Roman theologian and early Christian author; called "the Father of Latin Christianity"

Tosafot: Midieval commentators in the Talmud

Tur: 14th century Jewish legal code from composed by Rabbi Yaakov ben Asher, who is also known as the Tur

Yevamot: Talmudic tractate that includes many discussions about women, relationships, and conversion

Zohar: Foundational work of Jewish mystical thought of Kabbalah; its authorship to the attributed to 1st century Rabbi Simeon bar Yochai, but may have been written by Moshe de Leon in the 13th century

Havdalah: Literally, separation, referring to the ceremony and verbal declaration made at the end of Shabbat.

ABOUT THE AUTHOR

Rabbi Michael Barclay is an American rabbi, author, and lecturer. He is recognized as an insightful theologian who integrates authentic Jewish theology into 21st century situations.

The descendant of Ukrainian rabbis from Chernigov, Rabbi Barclay was both the Hillel Director and a professor in the School of Theological Studies at Loyola Marymount University in Los Angeles. He has lectured around the world on cross-cultural mysticism and meditation. Rabbi Barclay was also the recipient of the 2010 B'nai Zion Distinguished Humanitarian Award.

Rabbi Barclay is a frequent Torah commentator for *The Jewish Journal* as well as contributor for multiple periodicals including *The Jewish Forward*, *The Jewish Times*, *The Acorn*, and *PJ Media*.

In 2013, Rabbi Barclay founded the first non-Orthodox synagogue in the nation with no membership dues. There is no cost for High Holiday tickets, classes, and events such as lectures and concerts; and no financial costs for Bar/Bat Mitzvahs or tutoring. The full service synagogue subsists entirely on donations and grants. The synagogue is inclusive and non-denominational, using conservative prayer book

The temple is also the largest provider of free High Holiday services in the nation; and the only synagogue in California that never closed and never restricted live attendance during the Covid pandemic.

The majority of teachings and guest lectures are based on traditionally observant Jewish theology and Kabbalah. This inclusive theological practice and business model has been emulated around the country, starting a nationwide "movement" of synagogues with "no dues."

Rabbi Barclay has served as a peak performance coach for athletes and business executives seeking an extra edge in their field including Oscar and Emmy Award winners, NCAA athletes, CEOs of multiple corporations, and the Chicago White Sox.

He lectures across the world on Judaism, cross-cultural mysticism, and Jewish understandings of politics and ethics; and is brought around the globe to officiate life cycle events.

He is the author of two new books, both scheduled to be published in 2025: *Mirrors of the Heart: Finding, Creating, and Maintaining A Healthy Relationship* and *The Writings: Biblical Wisdom to Renew Your Spirit and Heal a Troubled World*